Zero Fux

(A Memoir)

*Healing Through the Cracks of My Past*

by

Justin Brooks

Copyright Page for Zero Fux

© 2024 Justin Brooks

All rights reserved. No part of this publication may be reproduced, distributed, or transmitted in any form or by any means, including photocopying, recording, or other electronic or mechanical methods, without the prior written permission of the publisher, except in the case of brief quotations embodied in critical reviews and certain other noncommercial uses permitted by copyright law.

ISBN: 979-8-9922227-0-8

First Edition

Printed in the United States of America

This is a work of nonfiction. The events, experiences, and recollections presented in this book reflect the author's personal perspective. Some names and details may have been changed to protect privacy.

# ZERO FUX

## Table of Contents

1. Introduction: The Shaded Light
   - Setting the stage for the journey and struggles.

2. Early Life and Foundations
   - Childhood experiences, family dynamics, and cultural influences.

3. Military Years: Structure and Chaos
   - Experiences in the Marine Corps, deployments, and personal struggles.

4. Josh: A Decade of Love and Loss
   - The beginnings, evolution, and collapse of a significant relationship.

5. Post-Josh and South Florida
   - Starting over, self-discovery, and early struggles with addiction.

6. Jack: Lessons in Love and Letting Go
   - A new chapter in love, breakups, and the foundations of independence.

7. Rehab and Reflection

- The first steps toward sobriety and the internal battles faced.

8. Rediscovering Identity
    - Reconnecting with family, heritage, and self-worth.

9. Life in Charlotte
    - Challenges, temptations, and the beginning of a downward spiral.

10. New Beginnings: United Airlines
    - Career aspirations, relapses, and fleeting victories.

11. The Breaking Point
    - Near-death experiences and the decision to seek help.

12. Lyons Rehab: A New Hope
    - Life-changing realizations and the journey toward recovery.

13. Sobriety and Rediscovery
    - Building a new life, navigating relationships, and regaining purpose.

14. Reconnecting With the Past
    - Revisiting family, cultural heritage, and old friendships.

15. Understanding Self-Worth
    - Recognizing value, breaking patterns, and

establishing new goals.

16. The Phone Call

- A full-circle moment, tying the past to the present.

17. Conclusion: The Road Ahead

- Hope for the future and a call to action for personal growth.

# **Preface**

My name is Justin, and I am an addict and an alcoholic. My life has been a roller coaster filled with winding ups and downs. This book is a shared and collective process that I hope will allow you to reflect on my journey through my feelings and experiences. I will do my best to convey my message honestly.

To tell this story, I had to go back many years. I have done my best to stay true to my perceived views and encounters to the best of my recollection. The following pages contain real names, real places, and real events. These people have no knowledge of what I have written until this time.

This journey began as a deeply personal healing process long before I shed light on my addiction. As such, this book will reflect changes in tone and structure as it progresses. While many of the relationships I've experienced had more good moments than bad, this book focuses on the extreme moments in my life during this period of culmination.

My intention is not to portray these individuals in a negative light or to cast judgment. Instead, this work reflects the experiences and emotions that emerged during my journey through addiction.

**Chapter 1: The Shaded Light**

The crashpad was buzzing with the usual chaos that came with sharing an apartment with eleven other flight crew members. It was a transient space—functional but devoid of comfort or permanence. The bunks, crammed together like a barracks, offered a thin veil of privacy with their makeshift curtains. But even behind mine, I couldn't escape the sounds of life continuing around me: hushed conversations, footsteps crossing creaky floors, and the clatter of coffee mugs in the kitchen.

My world, however, felt paused. I sat on the edge of my bottom bunk, staring at the small nightstand cluttered with evidence of last night's mistakes—a half-empty glass of vodka, a crumpled bag of cocaine. The remnants mocked me, reminding me that the party hadn't ended; it had just bled into another day.

My head throbbed, not from a hangover but from the crushing weight of my own thoughts. For years, I had crafted a facade, hiding the escalating spiral of addiction and isolation. But this morning, as the dim light filtered through the thin curtain, I knew I couldn't keep lying to myself.

I couldn't keep doing this.

Sliding the curtain aside, I stood up, my legs shaky as I made my way to the small bathroom. Cold water splashed on my face, and for a moment, I let the chill ground me. But when I looked up at the mirror, the reflection staring back was unrecognizable: bloodshot eyes, pale skin, a shadow of the person I once was. The sight was jarring, but it wasn't enough to break through the numbness.

I returned to my bunk and sat down heavily. The room around me buzzed with life, but I felt utterly alone. My heart pounded as I picked up my phone and scrolled through my contacts. My finger hesitated over her name: Mom.

Could I even say it? Could I admit out loud that I needed help?

For years, I had kept her at a distance, shielding her from the worst of me. Now, my walls were crumbling, and I was desperate for someone to help pick up the pieces. Taking a deep breath, I tapped the call button.

The dial tone buzzed in my ear, each ring amplifying my anxiety.

"Hello?" Her voice was the same as always—warm, steady, and somehow instantly comforting.

I froze. The words I had rehearsed in my mind vanished, leaving me fumbling.

"Hello? Is anyone there?" she repeated, concern lacing her tone.

"Mom," I croaked, my voice barely audible.

"Sweetheart? What's wrong?" Her response was immediate, her worry palpable.

"I—I need help," I whispered, my throat tightening as the admission hung in the air.

The silence on her end was brief but heavy.

"Where are you?" she finally asked, her voice soft but resolute.

"At the crash pad," I said, my voice cracking. "I—I can't do this anymore."

"Okay," she said firmly. "We're going to figure this out. You're not alone in this, honey."

Her words broke something in me. The tears came suddenly, hot and uncontrollable, as years of shame and pain poured out. I pressed my hand against my mouth, trying to stifle the sobs, but there was no stopping them.

"It's okay," she soothed. "Let it out. We'll get through this together."

For the first time in what felt like forever, I let myself believe her. I clung to the lifeline she offered, even as the fear of what lay ahead loomed large.

When the call ended, I sat there for a moment, letting the weight of what I had just done sink in. I had reached out. I had taken the first step.

Pulling out a duffel bag from under my bed, I began to pack. My movements were robotic, my mind a blur. A couple of roommates glanced at me as I passed through the common areas, but no one asked questions.

Stepping out of the crash pad and into the city streets, I felt the cool morning air hit my face. It was a new day, and for the first time in years, I felt a sliver of hope. I unlocked my phone and ordered a Lyft, standing on the curb as the minutes ticked by.

"Where to?" the driver asked as I climbed into the back seat.

I hesitated for a moment before replying, "East Orange Veterans Hospital."

As the car pulled away, I looked back one last time at the place that had been a shelter and a prison all at once. I didn't know what awaited me, but as the city streets blurred past, I held onto my mother's words: You're not alone.

The road ahead would be long and uncertain, but I had taken the first step. And that was enough—for now.

## Chapter 2: Early Life and Foundations

My early life was a tapestry woven with resilience, challenges, and fleeting moments of joy. It was in these formative years that the foundation for who I would become was laid—shaped by family dynamics, cultural influences, and a relentless need to survive in the face of adversity.

### *Childhood and Family Dynamics*

Growing up, my family was anything but conventional. My father was a strong figure in my early years, but the custody battle between my parents was a pivotal moment that fractured my childhood. After the separation, I found myself splitting time between two vastly different worlds—each one presenting unique challenges.

At my father's, there was a freedom that came with fewer rules, but this also meant there was little structure. Cigarettes, beer, and even adult content were normalized. He introduced me to work early, and I helped build his business while juggling school. These experiences instilled a strong work ethic, even as they blurred the lines between childhood and adulthood.

In contrast, my mother tried to create a more stable and protective environment for me, though I didn't realize it at the time. Her choices often left me feeling frustrated and misunderstood. While my father's world seemed freer, I now understand that my mother was trying to shield me from some of the chaos that could have unraveled me. Her actions, though imperfect, were rooted in love and an effort to provide a better path for me.

Despite her efforts, there were moments of strain. Money was tight, and trust between us was tested. At one point, she even took money I had saved, leaving me feeling betrayed and hurt. Yet as I matured, I began to see her struggles more clearly. She was navigating her own battles while doing her best to hold us together. Though it was not always easy to see, her unwavering love and determination to protect me remained constants in my life.

### *Cultural Influences and Latino Roots*

One of the most significant influences during my childhood was my cultural upbringing. Growing up in a community deeply intertwined with Latino culture, I was immersed in its traditions and values. My mother remarried, and my stepfather brought a different perspective into our lives. He was a Latino man with a quiet strength, and though I initially felt a sense of distance, his actions later taught me lessons in perseverance and respect.

Visiting my stepfather in jail as a child was a defining experience. It was a moment of confusion and disapproval from extended family, but it also highlighted the complexities of family loyalty. These visits were a stark contrast to the otherwise lively celebrations of culture that punctuated my upbringing. This duality of hardship and joy became a recurring theme in my life.

### *The Need for Independence*

From an early age, I realized the importance of independence. Whether it was mowing lawns to earn pocket money or taking on odd jobs to help out, I learned that self-reliance was key. My father's approach to life, while unconventional, taught me to fend for myself. My mother's love, though complicated, instilled in me a sense of resilience that would carry me through some of the darkest times.

Looking back now, I understand that while I saw my father's world as freedom, it often lacked the guidance I needed. My mother, on the other hand, tried to instill discipline and a sense of stability, even when I resisted. At the time, I couldn't see her intentions clearly. It took years of reflection to appreciate how hard she worked to shelter me from chaos and set me on a better path, even when I didn't recognize it.

The challenges of my early years left me with an undeniable drive to prove myself. While my family provided the roots, it was up to me to determine how high I would grow. These experiences would later shape the way I navigated relationships, career ambitions, and the quest for self-identity.

**Chapter 3: Military Years — Structure and Chaos**

The Marine Corps brought a semblance of structure to my life, but it also became a battleground for my internal struggles. It was a paradox: an environment that demanded discipline yet highlighted my deepest vulnerabilities. During my years of service, I was not only navigating the complexities of deployments and training but also grappling with my identity and the effects of growing up in a fractured family.

*Basic Training: The Start of a New Life*

When I first arrived at Parris Island, I was eager to prove myself. The grueling training, the constant barking of drill instructors, and the camaraderie among recruits created an atmosphere of both pressure and unity. I thrived in the structure, excelling in physical tests and learning to suppress emotions that could be perceived as weak.

Yet, even in this environment, my past haunted me. I carried the weight of my family dynamics—my mother's struggles, my father's absence, and the influence of a childhood marked by survival and adaptation. These feelings simmered under the surface, clashing with the newfound pride I was cultivating as a Marine.

## *Deployments and Fractured Focus*

Deployments brought their own challenges. The physical demands were immense, but the emotional toll was even greater. I found myself questioning my place in the world, torn between the expectations of the Corps and my own unspoken truths. It was during these years that I began seeking solace in unhealthy coping mechanisms—drinking to excess and avoiding introspection.

Despite the challenges, there were moments of clarity. Working long hours, I developed a strong work ethic that had been instilled in me during my childhood. Mowing lawns, building my father's business, and balancing school had prepared me for the relentless demands of military life. Yet, the structure I embraced externally clashed with the chaos I felt internally.

## *The Justin and Atlanta Incident*

During this time, I met Justin Scoggins, a man who introduced me to a world I had only tentatively explored. He invited me to Atlanta Pride, an event that marked a pivotal moment in my life. However, the weekend took a dark turn, culminating in a violent assault that left me hospitalized. The incident shook me to my core, forcing me to confront the dangers of my burgeoning identity in a world that was not always accepting.

The aftermath was a blur of emotions—shame, confusion, and anger. I sought refuge in my mother's home in Texas, where I turned to alcohol to cope. My relationship with Justin deteriorated, and I began to spiral. Despite the support of my command, who granted me additional leave to sort out personal matters, I struggled to reconcile my growing awareness of my identity with the expectations placed upon me as a Marine.

### *Coming Out in the Corps*

Returning to base after my leave, I was caught between maintaining appearances and being true to myself. Eventually, I reached a breaking point. During a meeting with my commanding officers, I admitted to being gay—a revelation that led to my separation under "Don't Ask, Don't Tell." While the process was emotionally taxing, it also brought a sense of relief. For the first time, I felt the weight of secrecy begin to lift.

### *Josh: A Beacon in the Storm*

Josh entered my life during this transitional period, offering a sense of stability I hadn't felt in years. He saw me for who I was and supported me unconditionally. Our connection deepened quickly, and I made the decision to leave the Corps and start a new chapter with him. Together, we began building a life, navigating the complexities of love, finances, and personal growth.

## Chapter 4: Josh: A Decade of Love and Loss

Josh was more than just a partner—he was my anchor for ten years. Our relationship saw incredible highs and devastating lows, shaped by moments of passion, betrayal, and personal growth.

### *The Beginnings: A Whirlwind Romance*

We met during a tumultuous time in my life. Fresh out of the military and recently discharged under "Don't Ask, Don't Tell," I was still finding my footing. Josh appeared like a beacon of stability, someone who saw me as more than just a veteran navigating an unfamiliar civilian world.

Our relationship moved fast. Within a month of meeting, I moved in with him. It wasn't planned, but it felt right. I was still grappling with the loss of my military identity, and being with Josh gave me a sense of belonging. He became my safe haven, a partner who seemed willing to build a life with me despite the chaos I brought with me.

### *Building a Life Together*

The early years with Josh felt like a dream. We settled into a rhythm, building a life that felt stable and full of promise. He encouraged me to pursue my dreams, and I tried to be the partner he needed.

But as much as I loved him, I leaned on him in ways that weren't always healthy. Josh became my emotional crutch, and I relied on his support to navigate my insecurities and fears. I didn't realize then that this dependency was planting the seeds for future challenges.

**The Seven-Year Fracture**

At the seven-year mark, the cracks in our relationship became undeniable. Josh had formed a close friendship with someone named Blake, and it quickly became apparent that this was more than just a platonic bond.

I could see it in the way he talked about Blake, the way his eyes lit up when he mentioned him. At first, I tried to dismiss it as paranoia. But the late-night texts, the inside jokes, and the subtle shifts in Josh's behavior told a different story.

Josh never admitted to having feelings for Blake, but he didn't have to. I felt it in every interaction between them, in the way he started pulling away from me emotionally. The seven-year breakup wasn't because of an outright betrayal—it was because Josh had emotionally checked out of our relationship.

When he told me he needed space, it felt like the air had been sucked out of the room. I was devastated, but I also knew deep down that he was right. We had become two people living parallel lives, holding onto a relationship that was no longer working.

I moved out and started over. It was one of the hardest things I'd ever done, but it also forced me to confront my own patterns of co-dependence and avoidance.

### The Second Chance

Seven months later, Josh came back into my life. He apologized for how things had ended, saying he had realized how much he missed me and wanted to make things right.

Against my better judgment, I gave him another chance. The idea of rebuilding what we had once had was tempting, and I still loved him despite everything. We tried to pick up the pieces, but things were never quite the same.

### The Ten-Year Collapse

By the time we reached the ten-year mark, the writing was on the wall. Josh had grown increasingly distant, and I was beginning to suspect that history was repeating itself.

Then, one night, I came home to find him in bed with Luke. It was the ultimate betrayal, a moment that shattered whatever trust we had left.

I stood there in disbelief, unable to process what I was seeing. Josh's pale face and Luke's unapologetic demeanor only added to the sting. They weren't just crossing a line—they were obliterating it.

After Luke left, Josh tried to explain himself, but there was nothing he could say to undo the damage. I realized then that our relationship had been over long before that night.

### *The Aftermath*

Walking away from Josh for the final time was both devastating and liberating. For ten years, he had been my partner, my confidant, and my best friend. Letting go felt like losing a part of myself, but it was also a chance to rediscover who I was without him.

The aftermath of our breakup wasn't easy. I struggled with feelings of inadequacy and self-doubt, questioning what I could have done differently. But over time, I began to see the breakup as an opportunity for growth.

### *The Lessons*

Josh taught me some of the most valuable lessons of my life. He showed me the importance of trust, communication, and mutual respect in a relationship—and what happens when those things are absent.

Our relationship, as painful as it was at times, shaped me into the person I am today. It forced me to confront my fears, break unhealthy patterns, and prioritize my own happiness.

Most importantly, it taught me that love isn't enough on its own. A healthy relationship requires effort, honesty, and a willingness to grow together. Without those things, even the strongest foundation will eventually crumble.

*Moving Forward*

As I look back on my time with Josh, I feel a mixture of gratitude and closure. He was a significant chapter in my life, one that taught me about resilience, vulnerability, and the importance of self-worth.

Moving forward, I carry those lessons with me. They've become the building blocks for the life I'm creating—a life defined not by past mistakes, but by hope, growth, and the promise of new beginnings.

## Chapter 5: Post-Josh and South Florida

When I left Josh, I wasn't just leaving a relationship—I was walking away from an entire life. South Florida was supposed to be my fresh start, a place to rediscover myself and put the pieces back together. But fresh starts aren't always as clean or simple as we imagine.

*Starting Over*

Moving to Fort Lauderdale felt like stepping into a completely different world. The energy was electric, the nightlife dazzling, and the sun almost too bright for someone in the middle of an emotional storm. I had transferred with Dillard's to a new store, a familiar anchor in the midst of so much change. It gave me a sense of purpose, something to focus on when the chaos in my head threatened to overwhelm me.

I found a small apartment in Davie, a modest place that was just far enough from the store to give me space but close enough to feel convenient. The process of setting up my new home was a bittersweet one. Every piece of furniture I bought, every wall I decorated, felt like a step away from the life I had known with Josh. It was liberating and heartbreaking all at once.

*The Struggles Begin*

Starting over wasn't easy. For the first time in years, I was truly on my own. I had spent so much of my life in codependent relationships that the solitude felt almost unbearable. There were days when I'd come home from work, sit on the couch, and stare at the walls, unsure of how to fill the silence.

It was during these moments of loneliness that I began to fall into old patterns. Addiction has a way of creeping back in when you least expect it, and South Florida was full of temptations. The nightlife was intoxicating—quite literally—and it wasn't long before I found myself leaning on alcohol to cope with the loneliness.

At first, it was just a drink after work, a way to unwind. But soon, one drink turned into two, then three, until I was spending more nights at the bar than at home. The vibrant social scene I had once found so alluring became a crutch, a way to numb the pain I wasn't ready to face.

### *Rediscovering Myself*

Amidst the struggles, there were glimmers of self-discovery. I started to build a new circle of friends, people who brought laughter and light into my life. Anna, who worked at the store with me, became one of my closest confidants. She introduced me to a community of people who, like me, were searching for connection and belonging.

Anna's friendship was a lifeline. She had a way of making even the darkest days feel a little brighter. Whether it was a night out in Wilton Manors or a quiet evening at her place, she reminded me that I wasn't alone.

Through these new connections, I began to rediscover parts of myself that had been buried for years. I started dancing again, something I had always loved but had abandoned somewhere along the way. I found joy in small things—sunsets on the beach, impromptu road trips, and even the occasional karaoke night.

### *The Turning Point*

Despite these moments of joy, the pull of addiction was always there, lurking in the background. There were nights when I'd look in the mirror and barely recognize the person staring back at me. I knew I was on a dangerous path, but I wasn't ready to admit it—not to myself, and certainly not to anyone else.

The turning point came during a particularly dark night. I had been out drinking with friends, and by the time I stumbled home, the weight of everything hit me like a tidal wave. Sitting alone in my apartment, I broke down. The tears came in waves, years of pain and self-doubt crashing over me.

At that moment, I realized something had to change. I couldn't keep running from my pain, couldn't keep numbing myself with alcohol and distractions. If I was ever going to truly start over, I needed to face my demons head-on.

*A New Beginning*

Leaving Josh and moving to South Florida was the first step, but it wasn't the end of the journey. It was a chapter of self-discovery, of learning to stand on my own and confront the parts of myself I had long ignored.

The road ahead was uncertain, but for the first time in a long time, I felt a glimmer of hope. I didn't have all the answers, and I knew there would be more struggles to come. But I also knew that I was stronger than I had ever given myself credit for.

This chapter of my life wasn't just about starting over—it was about finding myself again, piece by piece, and learning to embrace the person I was becoming.

## Chapter 6: Jack: Lessons in Love and Letting Go

Jack came into my life when I was at a crossroads. He was vibrant, ambitious, and unapologetically himself—a magnetic force that I couldn't help but be drawn to. When we first met, it felt like a whirlwind romance, the kind you see in movies. He had a way of making me feel seen and loved, and for the first time in a long time, I believed that I could have a healthy, stable relationship.

### *The Early Days*

In the beginning, everything with Jack felt effortless. We spent countless nights talking about our dreams, our pasts, and what we wanted for the future. He challenged me in ways no one else had. Jack wasn't afraid to call me out when I fell into old patterns of self-doubt or deflection.

One of the things I admired most about Jack was his passion. Whether it was his work, his hobbies, or the people he cared about, he threw himself into everything with his whole heart. He showed me what it meant to be present and intentional.

### *Building a Life Together*

When we decided to move in together, it felt like a natural progression. We found a small apartment in the city, a space that quickly became our sanctuary. Decorating it together was one of the first real tests of our relationship. Jack had a keen eye for detail and a clear vision of what he wanted. I, on the other hand, was more laid-back, content to let things come together organically.

It was during this time that I realized how different we were. Jack's attention to detail sometimes felt overwhelming, but it came from a place of care. He wanted everything to be perfect, not just for himself, but for us.

Looking back, those early days were some of the happiest in my life. We built routines, shared dreams, and started to envision a future together. But as time went on, cracks began to form.

### *The Beginning of the End*

The first signs of trouble were subtle—small disagreements that turned into lingering silences, moments of distance that neither of us addressed. Jack was always busy, his passion and drive taking him in a million directions. At first, I admired his ambition, but over time, it began to feel like I was playing second fiddle to everything else in his life.

On the flip side, I had my own struggles. I was still battling insecurities, still trying to find my footing after years of addiction and self-doubt. I relied on Jack more than I should have, looking to him for validation and stability.

The real turning point came when Jack started working with Loren, his business partner. Their connection was undeniable, and while I trusted Jack, I couldn't ignore the growing sense of unease. Loren was everything I wasn't—confident, polished, and seemingly perfect.

### The Breakup

When Jack told me he needed a break, it felt like the ground had been ripped out from under me. We had been arguing more frequently, the tension between us growing with each passing day. Still, I wasn't prepared for the moment when he sat me down and said he needed space.

At first, I begged him to reconsider. I tried to remind him of all the good times, of everything we had built together. But deep down, I knew that he had already made up his mind.

The days following our breakup were some of the hardest I've ever experienced. Jack and Loren moved out a week later, leaving me alone in the apartment that had once been our home. The silence was deafening, a constant reminder of what I had lost.

But amidst the pain, there was a strange sense of clarity. Jack's decision forced me to take a hard look at myself and my life. For the first time, I had to stand on my own two feet, without relying on someone else to prop me up.

*Lessons in Love and Letting Go*

Jack taught me many things, even in his absence. He showed me what it meant to love wholeheartedly, to give yourself fully to another person. He also taught me the importance of boundaries and self-worth.

Unlike my breakup with Josh, this one felt clean. There was no lingering bitterness, no drawn-out drama. Jack knew what he wanted, and while it hurt to accept that I wasn't part of his future, I respected his honesty.

In the months that followed, I began to rebuild. I found solace in my independence, rediscovered passions I had long neglected, and started to believe in myself again. Jack's departure, though painful, became a turning point—a moment that propelled me toward growth and self-discovery.

*Moving Forward*

Jack will always hold a special place in my heart. He was a chapter in my life that I'll never forget, a reminder of what it means to love and be loved. But he was also a lesson in letting go, in understanding that sometimes, the best thing you can do for someone is to set them free.

In the end, Jack's departure wasn't just an ending; it was a beginning. It was the start of a new chapter, one where I finally learned to stand on my own, to find value in myself, and to embrace the unknown.

## Chapter 7: Rehab and Reflection

Rehab was not where I imagined I'd end up, but it was exactly where I needed to be. Checking into the facility was both a moment of surrender and a spark of hope. I knew that my life, as it was, had reached its breaking point. Cocaine, alcohol, and years of self-destructive choices had left me depleted—physically, emotionally, and spiritually. Rehab wasn't just about getting sober; it was about rediscovering myself, addressing the pain I had buried, and finding a way to live without the crutch of addiction.

### *Facing Myself*

The first days in rehab were surreal. I had been so used to numbing my emotions that suddenly being forced to sit with them felt unbearable. I remember the first group session vividly: sitting in a circle of strangers, each sharing their stories of struggle and survival. It was both comforting and terrifying to hear how much we all had in common, despite our different backgrounds.

In the quiet moments between therapy sessions, I would retreat to my room and write. It became my outlet, a way to process the whirlwind of emotions that rehab was stirring up. One of the first poems I wrote was The Shaded

Light. It captured the duality I felt: the longing for the escape that drugs provided and the flicker of hope that maybe, just maybe, I could break free.

***The Shaded Light***

Have you ever sat there, cracked a smile, and then wanted to cry?

A thousand-yard stare—people hear you, but the words don't come out right.

Today I looked out the window, felt the sun, but still didn't want to be outside.

I was screaming, but smiles would peak, and I would breathe.

Today, I wanted coke.

I wanted to call up my guy and my friends and say,

"Can't wait to see you, be ready for the party favors."

But instead, I looked out another window and thought, "What happens next?"

Tomorrow is another day, another breath, another sunrise.

Another day to my first 30, even though... Today I wanted coke.

Writing this helped me confront the cravings head-on, acknowledging them instead of pushing them away. It was raw and painful, but it was also a step toward healing.

*Breaking Down the Walls*

One of the hardest parts of rehab was confronting the reasons behind my addiction. In therapy, I began to unpack the years of trauma and insecurity that had led me down this path. I talked about my childhood, my relationships, and the constant need for validation that had fueled so many of my choices.

I realized how much of my life I had spent running—running from pain, running from failure, running from myself. Rehab forced me to stop running. It made me sit still and face the truth: I had been my own worst enemy.

But it also gave me a chance to rewrite the narrative. I wasn't just an addict. I was a survivor. I had endured hardships that many people couldn't imagine, and I was still standing.

*Building a New Foundation*

Rehab wasn't just about breaking bad habits; it was about building new ones. Daily routines became anchors: waking up early, attending group sessions, journaling, and even learning to meditate. For the first time in years, I started to feel a sense of control over my life.

One of the most transformative exercises was listing my accomplishments. At first, it felt impossible. My mind was so used to focusing on the negative that I struggled to see anything good. But with the help of my therapist, I began to see the truth:

- I had survived combat.

- I had built a life with Josh, even if it didn't last.

- I had earned a degree and worked toward a master's.

- I had become a licensed flight attendant.

- I had checked myself into rehab, choosing to fight for my life.

This list became a turning point. It reminded me that I was more than my mistakes. I was capable of growth, of resilience, of change.

### The Road Ahead

As the days turned into weeks, I began to see a path forward. It wasn't clear or easy, but it was there. I started to dream again—not about the life I had lost, but about the life I could build.

I knew that rehab was just the beginning. The real work would start when I left, when I faced the temptations and challenges of the outside world. But for the first time in a long time, I felt ready. I had a sense of hope, a belief that I could do this—not perfectly, but one day at a time.

Rehab didn't fix everything. It didn't erase the pain or undo the damage. But it gave me the tools to start healing. It gave me a chance to rediscover who I was and who I wanted to be.

And for that, I will always be grateful.

## Chapter 8: Rediscovering Identity

After years of chaos, heartbreak, and addiction, the time had come to rediscover who I was. The journey wasn't linear, nor was it easy. I wasn't just trying to heal the wounds caused by broken relationships and substance abuse—I was also confronting the parts of myself I'd neglected for years. I needed to re-establish my identity, and to do so, I would have to reconnect with my roots, my family, and, most importantly, my self-worth.

### *Reconnecting With Family*

Family has always been a complicated word for me. I grew up straddling two worlds: my biological father's chaotic, permissive household and the vibrant, Latino influences of my stepfather's side. My parents' divorce had left me navigating these contrasting dynamics with little guidance.

At my father's, the structure was nonexistent. Cigarettes, beer, and even porn were normal fixtures of life in his home. Responsibilities were thrown at me, not as lessons in discipline or growth, but as necessities for the household to function. As a teenager, I worked tirelessly mowing lawns and even helping build my dad's business—all while juggling school. These efforts instilled a strong work ethic in me, but they also came with an underlying bitterness. I was left to figure out life on my own, without the guidance or emotional support I desperately needed.

On the other hand, my stepfather brought a different energy, one that was met with skepticism and disdain by my extended family. To my younger self, he represented a disruption, a change I wasn't ready to accept. My relatives' opinions shaped my perspective, and for years I harbored resentment toward him.

As I matured, though, I began to see things differently. My stepfather may not have been perfect, but he brought stability and care to our family during times when we needed it most. Reflecting on this as an adult helped me let go of the resentment I had carried for so long. It wasn't about honoring him or anyone else—it was about acknowledging the truth of my upbringing and finding peace in it.

### *Rediscovering Heritage*

Growing up, my exposure to my stepfather's culture had been constant yet peripheral. Spanish music would play in the background at family gatherings, and meals were often flavored with the spices and traditions of his heritage. But I never fully embraced this part of my life. It wasn't until I began reconnecting with myself that I felt the pull to explore my Latino roots.

Learning Spanish became a priority. I downloaded language apps and began practicing daily. At first, it felt like a chore—an obligation I had imposed on myself. But as the words started to make sense, as I was able to hold conversations and express myself in a new way, it became something much deeper. It was as if I was unlocking a part of myself that had been dormant for years.

In rediscovering my heritage, I also reconnected with memories from my childhood. I remembered the joy of sitting at the dinner table surrounded by family, the laughter and energy that filled the room. It was a reminder that even in the most complicated moments, there was love and connection.

### *Self-Worth: A Long-Overdue Realization*

One of the most profound parts of this chapter in my life was learning to recognize my own worth. For years, I had sought validation from others—partners, friends, even strangers. I had tied my value to how others perceived me, to their approval and affection.

Sobriety was a turning point. It stripped away the distractions and numbing agents, forcing me to confront the truth about myself. I realized that my worth wasn't something external—it was something intrinsic.

There were moments of clarity that hit me like a wave. During one therapy session, I was asked to list my accomplishments. At first, I couldn't think of any. My mind immediately went to the mistakes, the failures, the things I hadn't done. But as I sat there, the list began to grow: I had graduated boot camp. I had built a life with Josh, even if it hadn't lasted. I had been to combat and survived. I had earned my bachelor's degree and was only a few credits shy of a master's. I was a licensed flight attendant, working my dream job.

The list didn't erase the pain or the mistakes, but it reminded me of something important: I was resilient. I had faced challenges that many wouldn't have survived, and I was still standing.

*Moving Forward With Purpose*

Rediscovering my identity wasn't just about looking back—it was about moving forward with intention. I began to set boundaries, something I had rarely done in the past. I deleted dating apps, stopped seeking external validation, and started focusing on what truly mattered to me.

I reconnected with friends and family, reaching out to those I had distanced myself from during my struggles. These relationships became a source of strength and support, reminding me that I wasn't alone.

Most importantly, I began to dream again. Sobriety gave me the clarity to set goals and the determination to achieve them. I started planning a reunion with my foreign exchange family, something that had once seemed impossible. I thought about completing my master's degree, not out of obligation but because it was something I wanted for myself.

This chapter wasn't about perfection—it was about progress. It was about accepting who I was, flaws and all, and choosing to move forward anyway.

For the first time in a long time, I felt like I was truly living—not for anyone else, but for me.

*Chapter 9: Life in Charlotte*

Moving to Charlotte was supposed to be a fresh start—a new city, new opportunities, and a new chapter for Josh and me. But from the moment we arrived, the cracks in our relationship began to show. The excitement of our move was overshadowed by the tension that seemed to follow us. Looking back, Charlotte was less of a fresh start and more of a slow unraveling.

The house we rented was much larger than what we needed, a sprawling two-story with three bedrooms, two and a half baths, and two living rooms. Furnishing it became an immediate point of contention. Josh wanted everything done instantly, from furniture to decor, and seemed to look to Luke for ideas and validation rather than me. Every trip to a store turned into a fight, as if we were silently battling for control over a life that was already slipping through our fingers.

Luke's influence loomed large over our lives. He was more than just a friend to Josh—he was an escape, a confidant, and, as I would later learn, a temptation. I could feel the distance growing between us, but I ignored the signs, chalking it up to the stress of the move. In truth, I was the last one to know, the last one to accept that our relationship was no longer a partnership.

One day after work, I came home to find Josh mowing the lawn. It wasn't a big yard, certainly not as expansive as the one we had in Georgia, but it was still his domain. I sat shirtless on the porch, hoping to soak in the late afternoon sun, but his reaction took me by surprise.

"Are you just gonna sit there?" he snapped, barely looking up from the mower.

I was taken aback. I hadn't done anything wrong—or so I thought. Hindsight has a way of putting things into perspective, though. He wasn't angry because I was sitting there; he was angry because of everything we had become. Or, perhaps more accurately, everything we had failed to become. The life we had built together was disintegrating, and he resented me for it. He resented himself, too, but he couldn't—or wouldn't—say it.

We weren't a couple anymore. We coexisted, sharing the same house but not the same life. And yet, I didn't see it clearly at the time. I was so consumed by the idea of "us" that I couldn't fathom what it would mean to let go.

### The Beginning of the Downward Spiral

Charlotte offered a clean slate, but it also brought its share of temptations. The city was quieter than what I was used to—more suburban than vibrant. The nightlife didn't hold the same allure as it had in South Florida, and I found myself growing restless. Isolation became my enemy, and I turned to old habits to fill the void.

Josh, meanwhile, found solace in his growing friendship with Luke. They spent more and more time together, often without me. I tried to insert myself into their dynamic, but it was clear I was the outsider. The emotional betrayal was almost worse than the physical one I suspected but couldn't yet prove. I started questioning everything—my worth, my choices, my ability to make him happy. It was a dangerous spiral, one that pushed me further into my vices.

The nights become longer, the fights more frequent, and the love that once bound us together began to feel like a distant memory. We were no longer partners; we were competitors, each trying to outlast the other in a relationship that had already run its course.

### *Reflections*

Charlotte wasn't just the beginning of the end for Josh and me—it was the beginning of a new understanding of myself. For years, I had defined my worth through my relationships, sacrificing my own needs to make others happy. But as our life in Charlotte unraveled, I began to see the cost of that sacrifice. I wasn't living for myself; I was merely existing for someone else.

The move to Charlotte was supposed to be a fresh start, but it turned into a lesson in letting go. It was here that I began to realize the importance of self-worth, of standing on my own two feet, even if it meant walking away from the life I thought I wanted.

## Chapter 10: New Beginnings: United Airlines

Starting a new chapter at United Airlines in 2023 felt like a dream come true. It wasn't just about the prestige or the destinations—it was about proving to myself that I could still accomplish something meaningful despite everything I had been through. The uniform, the badge, and the responsibility carried a sense of pride that, for a moment, drowned out the chaos inside me.

Training was intense, but I thrived in structured environments. United's training program demanded focus and precision, and I threw myself into it wholeheartedly. It reminded me of boot camp in some ways—a rigorous schedule, expectations to excel, and a constant push to be better. Each day I passed felt like a small victory.

But small victories weren't enough to silence the demons. Addiction doesn't just vanish because you have something to look forward to. While I was physically present at training, mentally, I was fighting battles that my colleagues couldn't see. There were nights when I'd sit in my hotel room, fighting the urge to call my dealer. Sometimes I won. Sometimes I didn't.

Relapses weren't dramatic falls; they were slow, creeping descents into the familiar. A drink here, a bump there—just enough to keep the edges smoothed out without spiraling completely. At least, that's what I told myself. It wasn't long before I realized I was walking a tightrope, and the ground beneath me was cracking.

One of the hardest parts about working at United was the loneliness. The job was glamorous on the surface—flying to new places, meeting new people—but the reality was isolating. Layovers in cities where I didn't know anyone became opportunities to numb myself. The hotel bars, the empty mini-fridges, the silence of the rooms—they were all triggers. I started to understand why so many people in the industry turned to substances to cope.

The fleeting victories came in the form of connections. My colleagues were kind and supportive, even when they didn't know the full story. Passengers would thank me for my service, and for a brief moment, I felt like I was making a difference. Those moments, however small, kept me tethered to hope.

One layover in Denver stands out in my memory. I had just completed a particularly long flight, and the snow-covered city looked like something out of a postcard. I decided to take a walk instead of heading straight to the hotel bar. The crisp air cleared my mind in a way I hadn't felt in months. For the first time, I allowed myself to think about what I wanted—not just in my career, but in my life.

United Airlines was more than a job—it was a chance to rewrite my story. But I realized that if I didn't address the root of my struggles, no amount of success would fill the void. The question wasn't whether I could excel at work; it was whether I could confront the parts of myself that I had been running from.

## Chapter 11: The Breaking Point

The Breaking Point wasn't one singular moment, but rather an accumulation of near-misses, heartaches, and physical collapses that I could no longer ignore. It was a crescendo of chaos that had been building for years, starting with Josh, escalating with Jack, and finally exploding in my destructive solitude.

It began with the high of invincibility that comes with addiction. I was functioning—at least on the surface. I had a job, connections, and my routines. But deep inside, I was spiraling. Late nights blurred into mornings; the parties and drinking numbed me enough to pretend I was okay. My cocaine use had become so normalized that it no longer felt like a problem—until my body began betraying me.

In late July, I was coming back from Cancun, recovering from Dengue fever but not quite well. My body felt weak, my head clouded, but I thought I could power through. On that flight home, as I sat feverish and exhausted, I began to feel the toll of years of abuse. My tolerance for discomfort had been high, but now, even that was cracking.

When I finally landed and Jeff picked me up, I could barely function. My fever had spiked. I spent that night going back and forth between Jeff's bathroom and the bed, convinced I would vomit and collapse simultaneously. My mind, as always, wanted to reach for cocaine—to use it as a lifeline. But my body was rejecting everything, and for the first time, I realized I might not survive.

The next morning, Jeff urged me to go to the hospital. I refused at first, clinging to the idea that I could handle it myself. But the fever wasn't breaking, and I knew this was different. When the ambulance came, I felt both shame and relief. Shame for being so out of control, and relief that I was finally admitting I needed help.

At the hospital, they diagnosed me with Caribbean Malaria, something I had likely contracted during my trip to Cancun. My body was shutting down, weakened not just by the disease but by years of neglect. The doctors pumped me with fluids and sent me home to recover, but it wasn't just the Malaria that needed healing. It was everything else.

Over the next few weeks, I tried to resume life as usual, but my body and mind had reached their limits. I couldn't eat without feeling nauseous. My anxiety was through the roof. Even the sound of laughter from my housemates felt grating. I knew I needed to stop pretending I could handle it all.

Finally, on July 22, I checked into detox. I packed a bag, including my drugs—because I couldn't fathom leaving them behind. I planned to use until the very last moment. When I handed over my belongings at check-in, the nurse searched my bag but missed the cocaine. I continued to use while in detox, clinging to my habit even as my body begged for relief.

My last day of use was July 25, and my first day of sobriety was July 26—a date that holds profound significance because it's also my sister's birthday. The irony wasn't lost on me—a day of life and celebration marked the beginning of my journey to reclaim my own life.

Checking into rehab on July 29, my birthday, felt poetic. It was a rebirth of sorts. I was scared, angry, and lost, but for the first time in years, I felt a spark of hope. I wasn't just surviving—I was choosing to fight for my life.

## Chapter 12: Lyons Rehab: A New Hope

Walking through the doors of the Lyons Rehabilitation Center was both humbling and terrifying. It felt like stepping into a world I didn't yet belong to—a world where people were honest about their pain, their failures, and their hope for something better. For so long, I had hidden behind a mask of confidence and control, refusing to acknowledge the chaos that addiction had brought into my life. But here, there were no masks, no facades. Just raw, unfiltered humanity.

### *Confronting Myself*

The first days at Lyons were the hardest. Detoxing physically was only the beginning. The emotional and psychological detox—the unearthing of every buried shame, fear, and regret—was far more excruciating. I sat in group therapy sessions, listening to others share their stories, wondering if I could ever find the courage to tell mine.

When my turn came, I hesitated. How could I explain the years of addiction, the lies I had told, the relationships I had damaged? But as the words spilled out, I felt an unfamiliar sense of relief. For the first time in years, I wasn't carrying the weight alone. My secrets were no longer festering inside me— they were out in the open, met not with judgment but with understanding.

*Life-Changing Realizations*

One of the most profound lessons I learned at Lyons was that addiction is not just about substances. It's about the voids we try to fill, the wounds we try to numb, and the ways we lose ourselves in the process. I began to see my addiction not as a failure of willpower but as a maladaptive coping mechanism—a way to survive when I didn't know how to thrive.

The therapists at Lyons pushed me to confront the root causes of my addiction. They asked hard questions: What was I running from? Why did I believe I wasn't enough? Slowly, I started to piece together the answers. I saw how my childhood experiences, my relationships, and my own self-perception had shaped the person I had become.

One moment stands out vividly. During a one-on-one session, my therapist asked me to write down all my accomplishments. I resisted at first, dismissing them as insignificant. But as I wrote, I realized how much I had achieved despite my struggles. I had graduated from boot camp, built a house, survived combat, pursued higher education, and started a career in the airline industry. For the first time, I saw myself as more than my addiction. I was resilient, capable, and deserving of a second chance.

*Building Connections*

The connections I made at Lyons were unlike any I had experienced before. In this space, vulnerability was not a weakness but a strength. We shared our fears, our hopes, and our dreams. We held each other accountable and celebrated each other's progress. These relationships reminded me of the power of community—the way we can lift each other up when we feel like falling.

One particular individual, a fellow veteran, became a source of inspiration for me. His story mirrored mine in many ways, and his determination to rebuild his life gave me hope that I could do the same. We spent hours talking about our shared experiences, finding comfort in the knowledge that we weren't alone.

*A New Hope*

Lyons gave me something I hadn't felt in years: hope. Hope that I could heal, hope that I could create a life worth living, and hope that I could become the person I wanted to be. The tools I gained here—self-awareness, coping mechanisms, and the ability to ask for help—became the foundation of my recovery journey.

As my time at Lyons came to an end, I felt both excitement and trepidation. I knew the road ahead would be challenging, but I also knew I wasn't walking it alone. For the first time in a long time, I believed in myself. I believed in the possibility of change. And that belief was the greatest gift Lyons could have given me.

## Chapter 13: Sobriety and Rediscovery

Sobriety is more than the absence of substances—it's the rediscovery of self, purpose, and the ability to live life authentically. When I began my recovery, I knew I was stepping into uncharted territory. Building a new life meant confronting hard truths, navigating relationships with newfound clarity, and regaining a sense of identity that had been buried under years of addiction.

### *Building a New Life*

Recovery came with the challenge of rebuilding the pieces I had lost and finding new ones to fit into the puzzle of my life. Sobriety gave me the clarity to focus on my goals and aspirations. Dreams that once felt unattainable—like finishing my degree, reconnecting with my family, and establishing stability—started to feel possible again.

Simple routines became milestones. Cooking a healthy meal, waking up early to exercise, or even paying bills on time brought a sense of accomplishment I hadn't felt in years. I learned to celebrate these small victories, as they were stepping stones to larger achievements.

### *Navigating Relationships*

Sobriety also changed the way I approached relationships. Addiction had taught me to manipulate, hide, and numb. Recovery demanded honesty, vulnerability, and openness. These were skills I had to relearn, often painfully, as I reconnected with loved ones and attempted to form new bonds.

One of the most challenging aspects was addressing the relationships I had damaged. Apologizing for past mistakes, listening without defensiveness, and accepting that not everyone would forgive me was humbling. However, these conversations also brought healing and deepened connections with those who chose to remain in my life.

Romantic relationships posed their own challenges. In sobriety, I realized how much of my identity and self-worth had been tied to being needed by others. Learning to stand on my own and value myself independent of a partner was a hard-won lesson.

### *Regaining Identity*

Rediscovery became a central theme in my recovery. Who was I without substances? What did I truly value? These questions didn't have easy answers, but they guided me toward growth.

I began to explore hobbies and passions that had been buried during my years of addiction. Writing became a form of therapy and self-expression. I poured my thoughts into journals, capturing moments of triumph and struggle alike. Fitness became another outlet, not just for physical health but for rebuilding confidence and discipline.

Sobriety also allowed me to reconnect with the person I was before addiction took hold. I rediscovered my love for travel, my curiosity about different cultures, and my desire to learn. These pieces of myself, once overshadowed by my addiction, became the foundation of my new life.

### *Moving Forward*

Sobriety is not a destination but a journey. Every day presents new challenges and opportunities for growth. While I still grapple with moments of doubt and temptation, I've learned that each choice I make has the power to shape my future.

In rediscovering myself, I've come to see sobriety as a gift—not just for me, but for those I care about. It's a chance to show up fully, live authentically, and create a life that aligns with my values and dreams.

The road ahead may not always be smooth, but it's mine to walk. And for the first time in a long time, I'm excited to see where it leads.

## Chapter 14: Reconnecting With the Past

Life has a way of looping back to moments and places that shaped us, often in unexpected ways. When I began my sobriety journey, the past felt like a weight I couldn't ignore. Reaching out to my cultural roots and childhood connections became both a challenge and a necessity.

### *Revisiting Family and Heritage*

Growing up surrounded by my Latino stepfather's influence was a formative experience, even if complicated. As a child, I remember the warmth of family gatherings, the laughter that filled the room, and the blend of English and Spanish that danced in the air. Yet, there was always tension—a push and pull between what was expected of me and what I thought I wanted for myself.

My stepfather, while flawed, taught me resilience and work ethic. When I was younger, watching him visit relatives, even those behind bars, left an impression on me about loyalty and family bonds. But as I grew, I also felt the weight of my mother's disdain for him and the whispers of disapproval from extended family. I struggled with where I fit in that dynamic.

When I reached out to revisit these moments during recovery, I was met with a mix of joy and hesitation. My efforts to reconnect weren't always reciprocated in the way I'd hoped. Many memories were bittersweet—what once felt like unity had given way to distance and misunderstandings. Despite this, I began learning to find closure and appreciate the fragments of love and culture I could reclaim.

### *Old Friendships*

Reconnecting with my cultural heritage opened a door to reevaluating friendships from my youth. Yet, as I reflect on those moments, I realize how much time and distance can change us.

I had vivid memories of my foreign exchange family from high school, where I had a chance to experience life in another country. I promised myself I'd see them again as an adult, to fully appreciate the bond we'd created. Though I haven't managed to follow through on that dream yet, it remains a goal I hold close.

Friendships have always been pivotal in shaping my sense of belonging. During my addiction, many relationships faltered under the weight of my choices. But with time and sobriety, I've started reaching out—not just to rebuild but to honor what once was. Some friendships thrive again, while others remain memories, treasured but distant.

### *Rediscovering Myself*

In reconnecting with my past, I've realized that my journey isn't about perfect endings or neatly tied bows. It's about the attempt—the willingness to face where I've been and how it's shaped me.

While I haven't yet seen my foreign exchange family, or revisited all the places that hold pieces of my childhood, I know I will. Recovery has taught me that healing isn't always immediate or linear, but it's possible. And as I continue to rediscover my roots and relationships, I carry hope and gratitude for the road ahead.

## Chapter 15: Understanding Self-Worth

The journey to understanding self-worth is not a linear one. It's riddled with setbacks, revelations, and moments of profound clarity. For me, it was a process of peeling back layers of doubt, societal conditioning, and the voices of others that I had allowed to dictate my life for far too long.

### *Recognizing Value*

I spent so much of my life attaching my value to the opinions of others. Whether it was seeking validation from a partner, friends, or even strangers, my self-esteem seemed to hinge on external factors. It wasn't until I began stripping away those influences that I started to see my intrinsic worth.

The most eye-opening moment came during therapy at the rehab center. My therapist handed me a piece of paper and asked me to list all of my accomplishments. At first, I scoffed at the idea. My mind was clouded by the belief that I had failed in more areas than I had succeeded. But as I started writing, a different narrative began to emerge.

- I had graduated boot camp, something not everyone can claim.
- I had built a home with Josh—despite its eventual downfall, it was still a significant achievement.

- I survived combat and returned with my integrity intact.

- I earned a bachelor's degree and was just shy of completing a master's program.

- I worked hard to achieve a dream job as a flight attendant, navigating the rigorous training and licensing process.

For the first time, I saw my life from a lens of accomplishment rather than failure. It wasn't about what I had lost or where I had faltered; it was about the strength and resilience I had shown to get through it all.

***Breaking Patterns***

Understanding my worth also meant acknowledging the patterns that had kept me stuck. Time and time again, I had sought external validation, jumping from one toxic situation to the next, thinking the next relationship or achievement would complete me.

Breaking these cycles required painful self-awareness. I deleted the dating apps that had consumed so much of my time. I stopped romanticizing relationships that were never meant to last. Most importantly, I started practicing self-affirmations—something that felt foreign at first but gradually became empowering.

Every morning, I would look in the mirror and remind myself:

"I am enough. I am valuable. I am capable of giving and receiving love without compromising who I am."

***Establishing New Frameworks***

With this newfound understanding of my worth, my relationships began to change. I started setting boundaries—not just with others but with myself. I no longer tolerated disrespect or behavior that diminished my sense of self. I learned to say "no" without guilt and "yes" to opportunities that aligned with my values.

My friendships became deeper, more genuine. Instead of seeking people who could fill a void, I surrounded myself with those who celebrated my growth and encouraged my journey. The reunion with my foreign exchange family was a testament to this shift—they saw me for who I truly was, not just who I had been.

Romantically, I approached relationships with a new lens. I wasn't looking for someone to complete me; I was looking for someone to compliment the person I had worked so hard to become. The desperation I once felt to be loved was replaced by a quiet confidence in knowing I deserve the right kind of love.

*Final Reflection*

Understanding self-worth is not a destination; it's a lifelong journey. There are still days when doubt creeps in, when old insecurities rear their heads. But now, I have the tools to face them head-on. I remind myself of my accomplishments, my growth, and the unwavering truth that I am enough as I am.

**Chapter 16: The Phone Call**

It was New Year's Day, 2023. The morning was still, the light seeping through the windows of my Boston crash pad. I had just made myself a drink—a vodka soda, my usual—and sat in the living room. The apartment was quiet, a stark contrast to the year that had just passed. I was trying to settle into the day when my phone buzzed on the table.

Misty. Her name on the screen stopped me. We hadn't spoken much lately, but I always appreciated her directness and care. Still, something about the timing felt off. I answered, steadying myself.

"Hey, Misty. Happy New Year."

There was a pause on the other end, just long enough to make my stomach clench. Finally, she said, "I don't know how to tell you this."

I gripped the phone tighter and responded quickly, almost impatiently. "Just say it."

"It's Nocona," she said, her voice trembling. "He passed away last night."

***The Weight of the News***

I didn't respond right away. The words hung in the air, heavy and piercing. "He's gone." My brother, estranged since I was five, was gone. My mind raced, but my body felt frozen. It was as if the floor had dropped out from under me, leaving me suspended in a strange, numbing limbo.

Misty's voice broke through the haze, filling in the gaps with details I could barely process. As she spoke, my mind leapt to the inevitable: I had to tell my dad. The thought tightened my chest. Our relationship was already strained, but this would push it further. He had not been there when I needed him most, and now, in this moment of loss, I would have to deliver the news that would make him confront his absence.

### A Fractured Relationship

My relationship with my dad had always been complicated, marked by distance and disappointment. When I was young, I had watched him prioritize his needs and wants over being present for me. Those feelings of abandonment had hardened over the years, especially after Nocona and I became estranged. Now, with Nocona gone, I was faced with the uncomfortable reality of confronting those old wounds.

The weight of the responsibility fell squarely on my shoulders. I had to be the one to tell him, to navigate the emotions he would likely never express and the blame he might try to deflect. But at that moment, I wasn't ready. I wasn't even sure I could handle my own grief, let alone his.

## *Processing Loss*

After the call ended, I sat in silence. The untouched drink on the table felt like an anchor, pulling me down. My chest tightened as I thought of Nocona—not as the distant figure he had become, but as the brother I had once known. Flashes of memories surfaced: fragments of a childhood that seemed a lifetime away.

The grief hit in waves. I wasn't just mourning Nocona; I was mourning the relationship we never had, the time we had lost, and the chances we'd never get back. It was a strange kind of pain—raw yet distant, like an ache for something you never truly knew.

## *The Weight of Responsibility*

I called Misty back later that day. "I don't know how to tell Dad," I admitted, my voice shaky. "I don't even know where to start."

Her voice was calm, reassuring. "Just be honest. He needs to know, even if it's hard."

But honesty felt like a double-edged sword. How could I deliver such devastating news to a man who had failed me so many times? The resentment I carried for him boiled under the surface, threatening to spill over. Yet, at the same time, I knew this wasn't about me. It was about Nocona.

When I finally made the call, it was as difficult as I had imagined. My dad's reaction was muted, almost detached, as though he didn't quite know how to process the news. He offered no comfort, no words of support—just a quiet acknowledgment of the loss. It deepened the chasm between us, solidifying my sense that I would always be the one holding things together, even when it wasn't my responsibility.

### *A Turning Point*

Nocona's death became a turning point, though not in the way I expected. It forced me to confront not only my grief but also the unresolved pain I carried from my family dynamics. It made me question the roles I had been playing in my relationships—caretaker, peacekeeper, and sometimes scapegoat—and whether I was willing to continue carrying those burdens.

That day, I made a decision. I couldn't change the past, but I could change how I moved forward. I would honor Nocona's memory by living authentically, by reconnecting with the parts of myself I had neglected, and by letting go of the weight of others' expectations.

## *Full Circle*

Sitting in my living room that evening, I poured the vodka down the sink. It was a symbolic act, one that marked the beginning of a new chapter. For years, I had been numbing myself, avoiding the pain and complexity of my life. But now, I was ready to face it head-on.

The phone call from Misty wasn't just a notification of loss; it was a wake-up call. It reminded me of the fragility of time and the importance of healing. As I sat in the quiet of my apartment, I whispered a promise to myself and to Nocona: I would live—not just for him, but for me, too.

## Chapter 17: Conclusion: The Road Ahead

Hope is a quiet but persistent companion. It doesn't demand attention, but it waits for us to notice its presence, to reach out and grasp it. As I sit here, reflecting on all that has been, I find myself holding hope like a lantern—something to guide me forward, even in the darkest of moments.

This story, while deeply personal, is not unique. It's a reflection of what it means to be human: to falter, to break, and to rebuild. Life doesn't offer perfect endings or simple solutions. Instead, it presents us with opportunities to learn, adapt, and grow.

*A New Perspective*

The road ahead is uncharted, and I no longer fear that uncertainty. Instead, I embrace it with a curiosity that once seemed impossible. There's an empowering freedom in letting go of the need to control every outcome. For the first time, I'm not fixated on where I'll end up; I'm focused on how I'll walk the journey.

Sobriety has given me the clarity to dream again—not reckless dreams born from escapism, but thoughtful visions of a life lived fully and authentically. I've reconnected with the people and passions that matter most to me, and I've started to build a foundation that feels steady and secure.

I'm not naive enough to believe the road ahead will be free of challenges. There will be days when the weight of the past feels heavy and moments when self-doubt creeps in. But I've learned that those feelings are not my identity—they're simply passing shadows in the light of my determination.

### A Call to Action

To those reading this, I offer this: believe in your capacity to change, even when it feels impossible. Take one step, and then another. Whether your struggle is with addiction, relationships, or self-worth, know that you are not alone in your battle. The act of showing up for yourself is the bravest thing you can do.

Forgive yourself for the missteps. Celebrate your progress, no matter how small it may seem. Surround yourself with people who see your worth, and walk away from those who don't. Above all, remember that your value isn't tied to your past—it's rooted in your resilience and your ability to keep moving forward.

### Looking Ahead

The journey continues, and I am committed to walking it with intention. There are chapters of my life still unwritten, adventures yet to unfold, and lessons still waiting to be learned. I am not defined by what I've endured but by how I choose to rise from it.

This is not the end of my story—it's a beginning. A beginning filled with hope, determination, and the unwavering belief that life is a gift, no matter how messy or imperfect it may be.

So here's to the road ahead: may it be filled with growth, love, and the quiet courage to face whatever comes next. And to you, dear reader—may you find the strength to walk your own road with the same hope that has guided me.

Things I Learned During My Journey

1. The Power of Letting Go

- Life doesn't wait for you to perfect yourself.

- Embracing imperfection allowed me to finally move forward.

2. Strength Through Vulnerability

- Breaking down doesn't mean breaking apart.

- Sharing my pain gave others the courage to share theirs, creating bonds I never expected.

3. Failure Isn't the End

- I learned to treat failure as feedback.

- Every "no" shaped my resilience for the "yeses" I deserved.

4. How to Prioritize Self-Respect

- Saying no without guilt was one of the hardest—and most important—lessons.

- I owe myself the same loyalty I once gave others blindly.

5. The Illusion of Control

- Accepting that I don't control everything was liberating.

- Life flows easier when I stop gripping so tight.

6. The Beauty of Rediscovery

- Falling back in love with life required stepping away from people and careers that dulled my spark.

*What's Next?*

1. Living Unapologetically

- This next chapter isn't about being reckless—it's about being authentic.

- I'm focusing on actions that feel right to my core, not ones that merely look good on paper.

2. A Renewed Focus on Community

- Whether it's helping someone heal, sharing my story, or mentoring, I want my journey to lift others.

3. Building My Legacy

- It's time to define what Zero Fux stands for long-term.

**Rewriting Chapter One—Letting Go of the Perfect Timeline**

I always thought life would unfold a certain way: dream job by 25, marriage by 30, kids shortly after. But life laughed at my plans. By 36, I was picking up the pieces of a shattered relationship, a lost career direction, and a profound sense of grief after losing my brother. Letting go of this imaginary timeline felt like a failure at first, but it freed me to redefine what success looks like. Today, I measure it by how aligned I feel with my values—not arbitrary milestones.

*Embracing My "Zero Fux" Mentality*

"Zero Fux" isn't about not caring—it's about caring about the right things. The moment I stopped giving my energy to people who didn't reciprocate, jobs that drained me, and expectations that weren't my own, my life transformed. I stopped seeking validation from people who'd never see my worth and started asking myself, "What do I really want?"

**Embracing the Zero Fux Mentality. What Zero Fux Really Means.**

Zero Fux isn't about shutting out the world or pretending you don't care. It's about clearing the noise, standing in your truth, and refusing to compromise on what truly matters. For years, I gave too much power to things that didn't serve me—relationships that drained me, expectations I never set for myself, and situations where I dimmed my light to make others comfortable. Zero Fux taught me to reclaim that power.

- **Lesson One: Permission Comes From Within**

I don't need external approval to be myself.

For too long, I sought permission from others—permission to feel proud, to rest, to say no. Learning to say, "I am enough as I am," was revolutionary. I don't need validation to chase my dreams or live my truth.

- ***Lesson Two: Boundaries Are Love***

Boundaries were the hardest lesson for me to learn, but they became my greatest act of self-love. Setting boundaries wasn't about shutting people out; it was about protecting my peace and energy. If I don't respect my own time and space, why should anyone else?

- ***Lesson Three: Progress Over Perfection***

The Zero Fux mentality means showing up even when it's messy. I stopped waiting for the perfect moment, the perfect partner, or the perfect version of myself. Growth happens when we take imperfect steps every single day.

**The Reclamation of Self**

Zero Fux gave me the freedom to:

- Walk away from people who treated me like an option.

- Take risks in my career without fearing judgment.

- Prioritize my mental and physical health.

By letting go of the weight of other people's opinions, I created space for joy, creativity, and authenticity.

Building a Legacy: The Future of Zero Fux

What Does Legacy Mean to Me?

A legacy isn't about fame or fortune; it's about impact. It's about creating something that outlives you—a ripple effect that inspires others to step into their power. My legacy isn't about being remembered perfectly; it's about being remembered authentically.

How I'm Building My Legacy

1.     Creating a Platform for Growth and Healing

I envision Zero Fux becoming more than a personal mantra—it's a movement. I want to create a space for others to share their stories, learn from mine, and heal. Whether through speaking engagements, books, or workshops, my goal is to empower others to find their own "zero fux" mindset.

2.     Mentorship and Advocacy

Part of my legacy will be in the people I uplift. I want to mentor others, especially those navigating loss, career pivots, or personal reinvention. Sharing my story isn't just about catharsis; it's about creating a blueprint for those still figuring it out.

3.     Authentic Creativity

My work—whether it's through writing, public speaking, or creative projects—will always reflect my truth. I want to produce art and ideas that make people feel seen, heard, and inspired. Zero Fux is the vehicle for that expression.

4.   The Ripple Effect

If my journey inspires one person to walk away from a toxic relationship, pursue a dream they've been afraid to chase, or prioritize their mental health, I've done my job. A legacy isn't just about what you create—it's about what you spark in others.

**Living the Legacy Every Day**

Building a legacy isn't about grand gestures; it's about daily choices. It's in how I show up for myself and others. It's in the words I write, the boundaries I hold, and the courage I cultivate. My legacy is unfolding, and every day, I have the power to shape it.

~ Legacy isn't built in a moment; it's built in the moments we choose to live unapologetically.

www.ingramcontent.com/pod-product-compliance
Lightning Source LLC
Chambersburg PA
CBHW050456110426
42743CB00017B/3382